Discover Dogs with The American Canine Association

I Like Akitas!

Linda Bozzo

It is the mission of the American Canine Association (ACA) to provide registered dog owners with the educational support needed for raising, training, showing, and breeding the healthiest pets expected by responsible pet owners throughout the world. Through our activities and services, we encourage and support the dog world in order to promote best-known husbandry standards as well as to ensure that the voice and needs of our customers are quickly and properly addressed.

Our continued support, commitment, and direction are guided by our customers, including veterinary, legal, and legislative advisors. ACA aims to provide the most efficient, cooperative, and courteous service to our customers and strives to set the standard for education and problem solving for all who depend on our services.

For more information, please visit www.acacanines.com, email customerservice@acadogs.com, phone 1-800-651-8332, or write to the American Canine Association at PO Box 121107, Clermont, FL 34712.

Published in 2018 by Enslow Publishing, LLC.
101 W. 23rd Street, Suite 240, New York, NY 10011

Library of Congress Cataloging-in-Publication Data

Names: Bozzo, Linda, author.
Title: I like Akitas! / Linda Bozzo.
Description: New York, NY : Enslow Publishing, 2018. | Series: Discover dogs with the American Canine Association | Includes bibliographical references and index. | Audience: Grades K to 3.
Identifiers: LCCN 2017009081| ISBN 9780766091238 (pbk.) | ISBN 9780766091245 (6 pack) | ISBN 9780766091252 (library bound)
Subjects: LCSH: Akita dog—Juvenile literature.
Classification: LCC SF429.A65 B697 2017 | DDC 636.73—dc23
LC record available at https://lccn.loc.gov/2017009081

Printed China

To Our Readers: We have done our best to make sure all websites in this book were active and appropriate when we went to press. However, the author and the publisher have no control over and assume no liability for the material available on those websites or on any websites they may link to. Any comments or suggestions can be sent by email to customerservice@enslow.com.

Photo Credits: Cover, p. 1 cynoclub/Shutterstock.com; p. 3 (left) Stieber/Shutterstock.com; pp. 3 (right), 6 Alena Stalmashonak/Shutterstock.com; p. 5 Grossemy Vanessa/Alamy Stock Photo; p. 9 Grisha Bruev/Shutterstock.com; p. 10 © iStockphoto.com/aabejon; p. 13 (puppy) cynoclub/Shutterstock.com; p. 13 (collar) graphicphoto/iStock/Thinkstock, (bed) Luisa Leal Photography/Shutterstock.com, (brush) In-Finity/Shutterstock.com, (food and water bowls) exopixel/Shutterstock.com, (leash, toys) © iStockphoto.com/Liliboas; p. 14 Dorling Kindersley/Getty Images; p. 17 Trio Images/Photodisc/Getty Images; p. 18 Jne Valokuvaus/Shutterstock.com; p. 19 © iStockphoto.com/ChicoG; p. 21 Eliska Sestakova/Shutterstock.com.

Enslow Publishing
101 W. 23rd Street
Suite 240
New York, NY 10011
USA
enslow.com

CONTENTS

IS AN AKITA RIGHT FOR YOU?

Akitas are not best for first-time dog owners. They are better suited for homes that don't have other animals or young children.

The Akita was bred to protect.

A DOG OR A PUPPY?

Akita puppies can take longer to train than other breeds. If you do not have time to train a puppy, you may want an older Akita instead.

Akita puppies grow into large, powerful adults. Proper training is important.

LOVING YOUR AKITA

Your Akita will enjoy being with his family. Love your Akita by giving him a toy he can carry in his mouth.

EXERCISE

Akitas enjoy walks on a **leash**. Playing games, like **fetch**, will keep your Akita from becoming bored.

Since Akitas don't get along well with other dogs, visits to the dog park are not a good idea.

FEEDING YOUR AKITA

Akitas can be fed wet or dry dog food. Ask a **veterinarian (vet)**, a doctor for animals, which food is best for your dog and how much to feed her. Give your Akita fresh, clean water every day.

Remember to keep your dog's food and water dishes clean. Dirty dishes can make a dog sick.

Do not feed your dog people food. It can make her sick.

Your new dog will need:

a collar with a tag

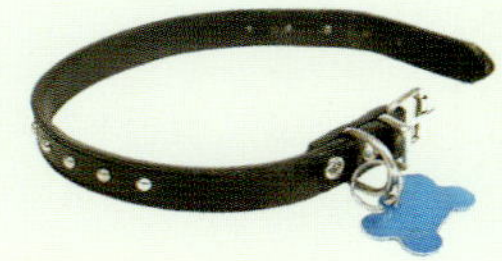

a bed

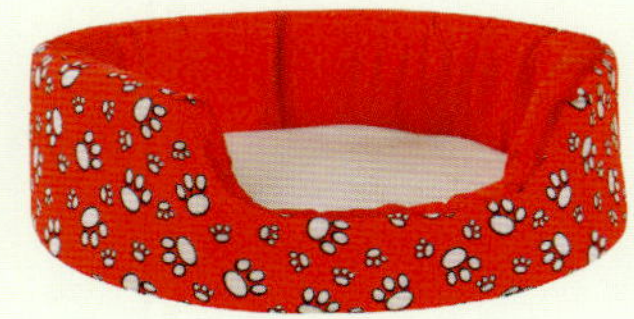

a brush

food and water dishes

a leash

toys

GROOMING

Akitas **shed** a lot. The Akita has two thick coats. Brushing your Akita will help keep him clean and free from knots.

Akitas do not need regular bathing. This can damage their coats. An Akita's nails will need to be clipped. A vet or **groomer** can show you how. Your dog's ears should be cleaned, and his teeth should be brushed by an adult.

An Akita will groom himself by licking himself like a cat.

WHAT YOU SHOULD KNOW

If bored, Akitas can get into trouble. They should not be left alone for long periods of time. Akitas make good watchdogs. They are quiet and loving when indoors.

You will need to take your new dog to the vet for a checkup. He will need shots, called vaccinations, and yearly checkups to keep him healthy. If you think your dog may be sick or hurt, call your vet.

A GOOD FRIEND

An Akita will be your friend for a long time. Akitas can live as long as 10 to 12 years.

NOTE TO PARENTS

It is important to consider having your dog spayed or neutered when the dog is young. Spaying and neutering are operations that prevent unwanted puppies and can help improve the overall health of your dog.

It is also a good idea to microchip your dog, in case he or she gets lost. A vet will implant a microchip under the skin containing an identification number that can be scanned at a vet's office or animal shelter. The microchip registry is contacted and the company uses the ID number to look up your information from a database.

Some towns require licenses for dogs, so be sure to check with your town clerk.

For more information, speak with a vet.

There are many dogs, young and old, waiting to be adopted from animal shelters and rescue groups.

Words to Know

fetch To go after a toy and bring it back.

groomer A person who bathes and brushes dogs.

leash A chain or strap that attaches to the dog's collar.

shed When dog hair falls out so new hair can grow.

vaccinations Shots that dogs need to stay healthy.

veterinarian (vet) A doctor for animals.

Read About Dogs

Books

Carney, Elizabeth. *Woof! 100 Fun Facts About Dogs.* Washington, DC: National Geographic Children's Books, 2017.

Mair, Cole. *Dogs from Head to Tail.* New York, NY: Gareth Stevens Publishing, 2016.

Murray, Julie. *Dogs.* Minneapolis, MN: Abdo Kids, 2015.

Websites

American Canine Association Inc., Kids Corner
www.acakids.com

Visit the official website of the American Canine Association.

National Geographic for Kids, Pet Central
kids.nationalgeographic.com/explore/pet-central

Learn more about dogs and other pets at the official site of the National Geographic Society for Kids.

INDEX